MONARCH BUTTERFLIES

Messengers of the Great Spirit

Raise them, Release them and Get your wish

By Martha Philbeck

Contact:
goldenpaws@embarqmail.com

http://authortree.com/MPhilbeck

Butterfly Indian Legend

If anyone desires a wish to come true they must first
capture a butterfly and whisper that wish to it.

Since a butterfly can make no sound, the butterfly can not reveal
the wish to anyone but the Great Spirit who sees and hears all.

In gratitude for giving the beautiful butterfly its freedom,
the Great Spirit will always grant the wish.

So, according to legend, by making a wish and giving the butterfly its freedom, the wish will be taken to the heavens to be granted.

To get your wish, why not help the Monarch grow up and then you can release many wishes to The Great Spirit.

The adult Monarch

The adults have a wingspan of about 4 inch and weight less that ½ ounce. They are easily distinguished by their color of brilliant orange reddish wings with black veins and white spots along the edges. The males have a black dot or stigmata along the veins of their wings. Below is a male that we hatched. Notice the black dot on the veins.

He is just about ready to fly.

The females do not have the black dot, but do have thickened black veins that show up.

THE ADULTS

Male Monarch: He has thin black veins with
Swollen pouches on the hind wings.

Female Monarch: the black
Veins are much thicker and there are
No hind wing pouches.

Lessons in raising Monarch Butterflies.

Every species of butterfly depends on a certain kind of plant to feed and grow. This is called a host. Milkweed is a host for Monarchs.

 Monarchs lay their eggs on the bottom side of a milkweed leaf and the caterpillars eat milkweed leaves to grow big and fat.

Milkweed gets it name cause when you break a leaf it secrets a white milky substance.

If you are raising Monarchs, you will have to keep a steady supply of leaves available. When the milkweed leaves dry replace them. The leaves will keep longer if the stem is wrapped in moist paper towels. Milkweed will stay fresh several days if kept in a closed plastic bag in the refrigerator. It can also be kept frozen for several months. It dries out quickly after being frozen.

In the fall the milkweed has seed pods that burst open and the fluffy seeds are carried by the wind. The seed pods can be dried and used for decorating. I have painted scenery on the inside of them for Christmas decorations. They are also used for fall decorations.

Notice how the pod is split to let the seeds float out. The plants grow from seed or the roots of last years plants. They grow a lot around fence rows in the fields or on the road sides.

The egg is on the leaf half on the left. It is the tiny white dot barely visible about halfway down. You may have to use a magnifying glass to see it in the picture. It is shaped like a football, flat on one end and has ridges. It is about 2 millimeters long. A monarch will only lay a single egg on a leaf. It takes an egg one to 12 days to hatch, depending on the weather. Eggs are hard to find in the wild.

The egg will turn dark when it is ready to hatch. A new caterpillar is tiny about ¼ inch long and the size of a thread. They are so tiny they are hard to see.

The tiny worm is on the left side of the leaf. It is just above the hole in the leaf. You may have to get a magnifying glass to see it and the egg, they are so small. This is also a good view of a milkweed.

The worms eat almost constantly so they have to have fresh milkweed leaves everyday. They create droppings almost constantly which will have to be cleaned out.

As they grow they shed their skin. They will shed it several times before they are grown.

Monarchs don't taste good. Toxins in the milkweed make them poisonous to birds and small animals. Milkweed is the only thing the larvae can eat.

It takes from caterpillar to chrysalis 10 to 12 days. They will start looking for a place to attach to. You can place a stick propped up in one end. We raise ours in an aquarium with a screen on the top. The caterpillars will climb to the top and attach itself to the screen. It will form itself in a hanging j. Then it will be time for its transformation into a chrysalis.

This worm is just attaching itself to the screen. Then it will hang in a j form before it turns into a chrysalis. To do this the caterpillar unzips its skin, wiggles and becomes the chrysalis. This is where the butterfly grows. The chrysalis is a beautiful jade green with gold dots. It is pretty enough to be a jewel. They attach themselves head down.

The Monarch chrysalis is one of nature's most beautiful creations.

The larvae will molt several times. When they get ready to molt they will get very still, often on the top or side of the container. The black head capsule will come off. Just after they molt their tentacles will look droopy and you might see the old skin behind them. They eat this skin.

This picture shows the different stages, it has the worm, several chrysalis and then the clear shell as the butterfly is starting to hatch.

The chrysalis will turn clear in 10 days. It will be clear for 2 or 3 days. Then the day it will hatch you can see the folded wings of the monarch. Watch closely or you will miss the magical show of the butterfly bursting forth. It happens very fast. The thin case bursts open and the butterfly emerge.

This picture is a very good illustration of how clear the chrysalis gets. Notice the folded wings of the butterfly still inside. This one was ready to hatch any minute.

The following pages are showing the different stages of hatching. Breaking free of the chrysalis, a Monarch greets the world. The clear shell of the chrysalis splits and quickly the monarch slips out to greet the world. It immediately begins to inflate its wings with the fluid contained in its swollen stomach. By moving its wings back and forth, it forces the fluid into the wings. It will take them several hours to stiffen and dry so that it can fly. As the wings inflate the body of the butterfly will take on more normal proportions. Any excess fluid will be expelled and then it will rest. After the wings stiffen and dry it is ready to take its first flight.

Notice the clear chrysalis from where another butterfly had hatched. The hatching is very fast.

It is sliding out very carefully to join the world. It makes you wonder how anything this size will fit into the chrysalis as small as it is.

Notice how small the wings are when they first hatch and how large the stomach portion is. As they flap their wings, it forces the fluid in the stomach into the wings and makes them grow.

See how swollen the belly is and how clumsy it looks. The Monarch is one of the most beautiful butterflies in nature. Their habitat is slowly slipping away. Milkweed is getting harder to find. It can grow from seed or the roots.

Each adult butterfly lives about 4 to 5 weeks. As fall approaches they have a special generation of butterflies that are born. This generation lives a whole lot longer than previous generations. These migratory butterflies survive 7 or 8 months. This generation flies to the center of Mexico for the winter. Then they begin their northward journey. When they reach the United States they begin to lay their eggs again. As the eggs hatch, these offspring only live 4 to 5 weeks. They will continue to move north, hatching and laying more eggs as they continue their northward journey through the United States to Canada.

Over the years we have raised many of these beautiful creatures. Each one is just as exciting as the last to watch hatch. The temperature should be no colder than 60 degrees when you release them. If they hatch in the morning it is ok to release them that afternoon. If they hatch in the afternoon keep them until the next day.

Place your finger in front of them and let them crawl onto your finger. You can carry them around.

The adult butterflies do not need to be fed until the day after they emerge. Then they will need to be fed daily. They eat a variety of food. You can place fresh cut flowers in containers, a small dish or jar lid containing a sponge saturated with a 20% honey/water solution. They will suck the juice of fresh fruit such as watermelons, honeydew or cantaloupe melons. Just cut them and set them in the cage. These have to be changes daily to prevent fermentation. Juicy juice from the grocery can also be used. You may have to put the front feet of the butterfly in the nectar and try to get him to unwind his tongue or proboscis into the food.

Life Cycle of

Monarch in

Pictures

Free at last

Swollen belly

Wings Inflated

Breaking free

Ready to
hatch

Notice the
gold dots

Starting to
go into chrysalis

Worm
Attaching

Butterfly Anatomy

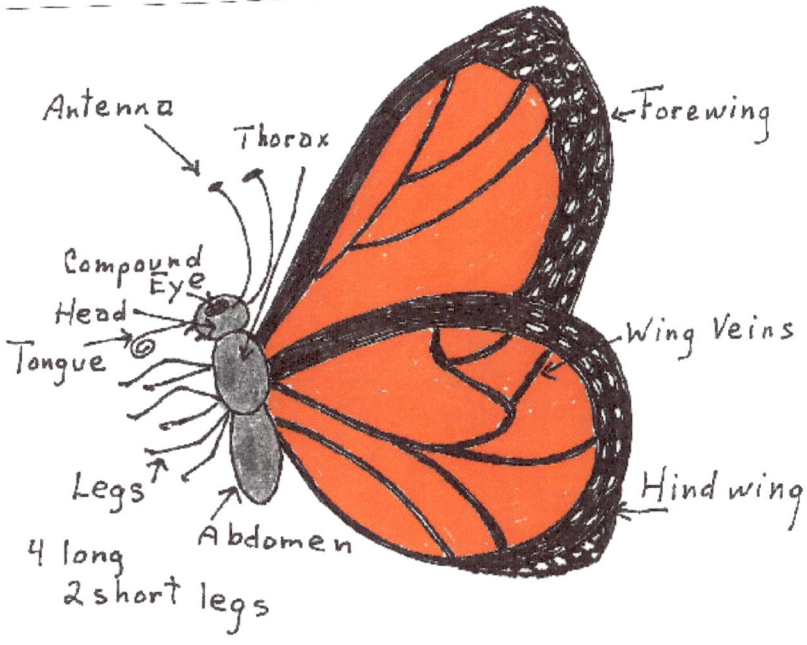

Antenna

Thorax

Forewing

Compound
Eye

Head

Tongue

Wing Veins

Legs

Abdomen

Hind wing

4 long
2 short legs

They have a long tongue or proboscis that curls up under the eyes and is used to reach in flowers for nectar or touch food for nourishment.

They have a long tubular heart that circulates the blood for nourishment.

There are 9 sets of breathing holes on the sides of its body called spiracles.

Food is stored in body fat.

They have an anus for the excretion of waste.

There is an organ at the base of the antenna that controls their balance when flying. It's called the Johnson organ.

Their wings are covered with small scales.

CATERPILLAR ANATOMY

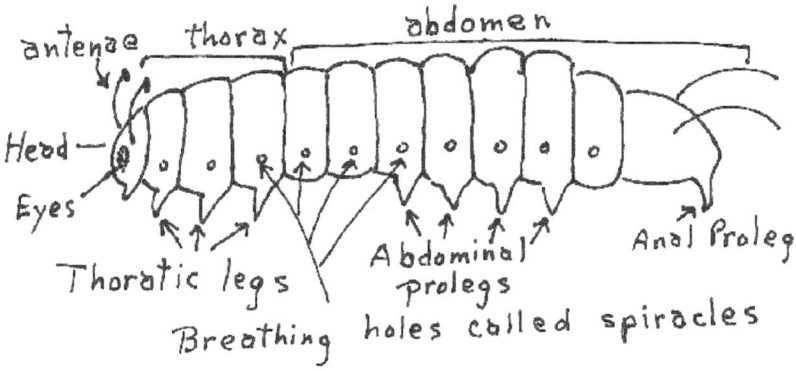

Caterpillars are the larval stage of butterflies and moths. They hatch from a tiny egg and then spend a lot of time eating and growing. As their skin gets tight they will shed it and grow a new one. Then they go into a protective shell while their body goes through a complete change. The body of the caterpillar is divided into 3 parts, the head, thorax and the abdomen.

The eyes are located on each side of the head. The mouth and jaws are also located there. Sensory hairs are located all over its body giving it a sense of touch. It breaths through holes in its side called spiracles. The 6 prolegs attached to the thorax will become the legs of the butterfly and the other prolegs will disappear in the adult stage.

The differences between a moth and a butterfly

- Butterflies are most active during the day.

- Wings are usually colorful

- Wings are upright when at rest

- They have a thin, hairless body

- Makes a chrysalis

- Antennae have a knob on the end

Moths

- Most active at night

- Wide, furry body

- Makes a cocoon

- Antennae are thick and feathery

- Wings are usually dull

- Wings are horizontal when at rest

Things that are the same

- Is an insect

- Has 6 legs

- Has 2 antennae

- Has compound eyes

- Has a 3 part body

- Has a proboscis (tongue)

- Have 2 pairs of wings

- Hatches from an egg

- Undergoes complete metamorphosis